Asian eleph..

African elephant

They have the biggest noses in the world

Baby elephants swing their little trunks around until they learn what to do with them. After a year, an elephant works out how to eat and drink with its strange, long nose.

African elephant

trunk

giraffe

zebra

They use it to smell, breathe, drink and delicately pick things up. They use it like a trumpet to make a noise – and even snorkel with it!

hippopotamus

African pear tree

western lowland gorillas

SHOW YOU LOVE AN ELEPHANT

Buy paper made from recycled elephant poo! Look online to find some.

African forest elephant

② They are good gardeners

Forest elephants eat seeds that pass through their bodies and out when they poo. The seeds start to grow in their dung.

So as elephants travel in search of food and water, they take seeds to new places and this helps the forests flourish.

great blue turaco

poo

3 They can talk with their feet

Elephants stamp their feet to say something. They might be sounding an alarm, excited about a storm or they might just be saying 'hello'. Miles away, other elephants feel the ground wobble and get the message.

baobab tree

African elephants

foot stomp

When they are excited, angry or scared, they also blow their trumpets. But mostly, elephants talk to each other with a low, rumbling noise that they make with their trunk.

herd of antelope

They know Granny's in charge

Female elephants and their calves stick together. The elephant in charge is the oldest female elephant. She remembers where to find food and water and knows her herd.

grandmother elephant

waterhole

dry, cracked eart

The oldest female remembers naughty elephants, helpful elephants, big elephants and small elephants. She always remembers if elephants or people she meets are kind or unkind.

African savannah elephants

scorpion

desert beetle

5 They have cool ears

Elephants flap their big, thin ears to help keep themselves cool. If they feel threatened, they spread their ears out to look really big and scary.

flapping ears

African bush elephants

They also use their huge ears to listen out for thunderstorms hundreds of miles away. If they hear rain in the distance, they head towards the storm to find a drink.

egret

spread-out ears

grasses

lion cub

lion

Indian
swallowtail
butterfly

orchid

SHOW YOU LOVE AN ELEPHANT

Adopt an
elephant! Find an
organisation that
helps to protect
them.

6 They cuddle and care

Baby elephants are playful and clumsy. Their mothers curl their trunks around them to keep them safe. All the grown-up elephants in the herd help look after the little elephants.

Elephants help each other out of trouble and wrap their trunks around each other in warm greetings. They understand how other elephants feel.

Asian elephants

mother

elephant calf

7 They are very clever

Elephants are one of the most intelligent animals on Earth. They solve problems by using tools like sticks to scratch and branches to swat at flies.

scratching stick

Elephants feel sadness and can get upset when a friend dies. If they find elephant bones, they gently stroke them with their trunks.

orangutan

Bengal tiger

fly swatter branch

SHOW YOU LOVE AN ELEPHANT

Be clever and fill your brain with elephant facts! Elephants have the biggest brains of any animal on land.

Asian elephants

8 They have giant teeth

Elephant tusks are actually very big teeth. They are made of a hard material called ivory. Elephants need their strong tusks to dig for water and food, strip bark from trees and go into battle. They can even be left or right-tusked.

acacia tree

antelope

curved tusks

African elephants

secretary bird

Poachers kill elephants for these spectacular teeth. They sell the ivory for lots of money. This is why elephants are in danger.

ostrich

stripped bark

SHOW YOU LOVE AN ELEPHANT

Don't buy things made from ivory! Thousands of elephants are killed each year for the ivory trade.

spongy
cushion

flower

red-cheeked
squirrel

9 They walk on tip toes

Elephants balance their heavy bodies on their toes. They have foot cushions like high heels inside their feet.

swallowtail
butterfly

leg

African
elephant

toenails

This spongy padding means
elephants walk very gently
and quietly, hardly making
any noise at all.

10 Their journeys never end

Elephants are always slowly wandering, travelling thousands of miles over their lifetimes. They remember where they can drink and keep cool. They cross rivers and huge areas in their endless search for food.

SHOW YOU LOVE AN ELEPHANT

Choose fair trade presents! They come from places where people make space for wildlife like elephants.